This book is dedicated to my precious Sarah, who has taught me of God's humor as well as of His love.

Edited by Aileen Andres Sox
Designed by Dennis Ferree
Art by Mary Rumford
Typeset in 14/18 Weiss

ISBN: 0-8163-1092-0

92 93 94 95 96 • 5 4 3 2 1

God
and Joseph
and Me

By Linda Porter Carlyle   **Illustrated by Mary Rumford**

Pacific Press Publishing Association
Boise, Idaho
Oshawa, Ontario, Canada

Joseph is my cat. We found him one day all alone beside the road. Mama said a busy road is a dangerous place for a kitten. We rescued him.

Sometimes I sit on the couch and hold Joseph and think about how glad I am that we found him and brought him home.

Papa says that's like what God did. God came to save me from this sinful and dangerous world. Someday very soon God will take me to His home. I will sit on His lap, and we will talk about how glad we are that He rescued me.

 feed Joseph in the morning. He likes to eat. He says, "Meow! Meow!" It means, "Hurry up. I'm hungry!" He is not very patient. I give him cat food and water. He likes it.

 like to eat too. I say, "Mama, what's for breakfast?"
She gives me cereal or eggs or pancakes. I eat it all.
I'm glad she never gives me cat food and water!

Joseph likes to play with balls of crumpled paper. He bats them across the floor and chases them. Sometimes he hides from his paper ball.

He crouches down behind the table leg and wiggles his bottom. Then he pounces. I like to watch Joseph play. He makes me laugh.

 like to play too. I like to run and jump and holler and ride my scooter as fast as the wind. I like to swing and touch the tree leaves with my toes. God likes to watch me play. I make Him laugh.

Joseph licks his feet to get them clean. He licks his fur all over. Papa says Joseph is a very fastidious cat. I think that means he doesn't like to be dirty.

am not fastidious. I like dirt. If I lick my hands to clean them, Mama says, "Stop that!" I wonder what she would say if I licked my feet?

ometimes Joseph sleeps all curled up in a little soft ball. He tucks his nose under his front paw. He makes little sleeping noises. Sometimes Joseph sleeps sitting up. He closes his eyes slowly and just sleeps sitting up. I like to watch him when he's sleeping. I smile.

ometimes I sleep all curled up in a ball. Sometimes I sleep with my feet peeking out from under the blankets. I wonder if I make little sleeping noises. God likes to watch me when I am sleeping. He smiles.

oseph knows he belongs to me. When I go outside, he cries at the door to go outside too. When I take a bath, he sits on the rug beside the tub. When I go to bed, he curls up beside me. I love Joseph! I think he's beautiful. I think he's funny. I love him even when he's naughty.

apa says now I know how God feels. Papa says God loves me even more than I love Joseph. God thinks I'm beautiful. God thinks I'm funny. And God loves me even when I'm naughty.

 love Joseph and Joseph loves me and I love Joseph forever.

And God loves me and I love God and God loves me forever and ever.

Parent's Guide

Ways to Share God's Love With Your Child

God and Joseph and Me was written to show God's unconditional love to your child in a way he or she can understand. The book is a tool you can use to talk about God's love with your child, a love God has chosen to give your child first through you—a human parent. Your love will represent God's love to your child. The hints in this parent's guide will help you demonstrate more of God's love in your home.

❖ Tend to your own relationship with God. What you learn about God's love will flow out from you to your child. A good place to start is by reading all the texts you can find in the Bible about God's love.

❖ Help your child believe in a smiling, loving God. If Jesus lived on earth today, He would hug your child and play with him or her. Help your child think ahead to the time he or she will play with Jesus in heaven by talking together about the picture on the previous page.

❖ Make worship time happy. Cuddle your child beside you or on your lap while you read Bible stories or a child's devotional book. Talk briefly about the good things God did for you today. Talk about the requests you want to make in prayer. Keep a family prayer journal in which you record God's blessings, your prayer requests, and the answers. Read through the book from time to time.

❖ Let your child catch you praying out loud. Ask God for help or thank Him as small things come up during the day. Thus you can teach your child to rely on a God who is always present, always willing to listen and help. Close your prayers with "We [or I] love You, Jesus."

❖ Spend time with your child. Give your child your full attention when you talk together. That means stopping what you are doing, establishing eye contact, and responding. Make Psalm 116:1, 2 your blueprint for listening to your child: "I love the Lord because he hears my prayers and answers them. Because he bends down and listens, I will pray as long as I breathe!" (Living Bible).

Linda Porter Carlyle and Aileen Andres Sox

Books by Linda Porter Carlyle

I Can Choose
A Child's Steps to Jesus
God and Joseph and Me
Rescued From the River!
Grandma Stepped on Fred!
Max Moves In